anythink

D0536051

Pebble®
Plus

>DESTRUCTION≪

CRUSH IT!

by Thomas Kingsley Troupe

Consulting Editor: Gail Saunders-Smith, PhD

CAPSTONE PRESS
a capstone imprint

Pebble Plus is published by Capstone Press,
1710 Roe Crest Drive, North Mankato, Minnesota 56003
www.capstonepub.com

Library of Congress Cataloging-in-Publication Data
Troupe, Thomas Kingsley.
  Crush it! / by Thomas Kingsley Troupe.
     p. cm.—(Pebble plus. Destruction)
  Audience: 006-008.
  Audience: K to grade 3.
  Summary: "Large, colorful photos and simple text illustrate vehicles being crushed at a salvage yard"—Provided by
publisher.
  Includes bibliographical references and index.
  ISBN 978-1-4765-2088-9 (library binding)—ISBN 978-1-4765-3489-3 (ebook pdf)
  1. Automobiles—Scrapping—Juvenile literature. 2. Crushing machinery—Juvenile literature. I. Title.
  TD797.5.T76 2014
  629.22'9—dc23   2013002441

Editorial Credits
Erika L. Shores, editor; Heidi Thompson, designer; Marcie Spence, media researcher; Sarah Schuette, photo shoot direction;
Marcy Morin, studio scheduler; Kathy McColley, production specialist

Photo Credits
Capstone Studio: Karon Dubke, back cover, all interior; Shutterstock: Huguette Roe, front cover.

Capstone Press thanks French Lake Auto Parts, Annandale, Minnesota, for providing the location
for the photography in this book.

Note to Parents and Teachers

The Destruction set supports social studies standards related to science, technology, and
society. This book describes and illustrates crushing cars. The images support early readers in
understanding the text. The repetition of words and phrases helps early readers learn new words.
This book also introduces early readers to subject-specific vocabulary words, which are defined in
the Glossary section. Early readers may need assistance to read some words and to use the Table of
Contents, Glossary, Read More, Internet Sites, and Index sections of the book.

Printed in China by Nordica.
0413/CA21300494
032013   007226NORDF13

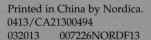

Table of contents

At the Scrap Yard

Old, broken down cars

fill the huge scrap yard.

Workers take off good parts
and tires from the cars.
The parts can be reused
or recycled.

Crush Time

A big forklift hauls the old car.

It sets the car inside

the crusher.

Start the crusher.

It's time to crush some cars!

The crusher mashes
cars nice and flat.

Let's keep crushing cars!
Even big vehicles like
pickup trucks get smashed.

15

The truck's metal crumples
and folds inside the crusher.

Crushed cars are stacked
like pancakes.
Workers will crush
more old cars soon.

Haul It Away

Semi trucks haul away
the crushed cars. The metal
will be recycled to build
something new.

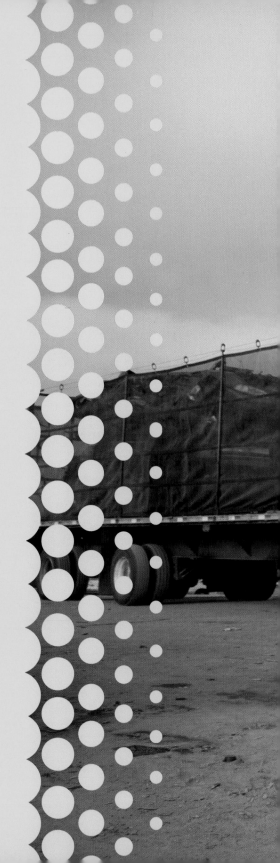

Glossary

crumple—to wrinkle and fold

forklift—a vehicle with two prongs or forks at the front, used for lifting and carrying loads

haul—to use a vehicle to move or carry something

recycle—to make used items into new products

scrap yard—a place where old and worn out vehicles go

vehicle—something that carries people or goods from place to place

Read More

Alinas, Marv. *Forklifts.* Machines at Work. Mankato, Minn.: A Child's World, 2007.

Steggall, Susan. *The Life of a Car.* New York: Henry Holt and Co., 2008.

Zemlicka, Shannon. *From Iron to Car.* Start to Finish. Minneapolis: Lerner Publications Co., 2013

Internet Sites

FactHound offers a safe, fun way to find Internet sites related to this book. All of the sites on FactHound have been researched by our staff.

Here's all you do:

Visit *www.facthound.com*

Type in this code: 9781476520889

Super-cool stuff!
Check out projects, games and lots more at
www.capstonekids.com

Index

Word Count: 106
Grade: 1
Early-Intervention Level: 14